JULIETTE G S0-BCR-161

AMERICA'S FIRST GIRL SCOUT

About the WOMEN OF OUR TIME® Series

Today more than ever, children need role models whose lives can give them the inspiration and guidance to cope with a changing world. *WOMEN OF OUR TIME*, a series of biographies focusing on the lives of twentieth-century women, is the first such series designed specifically for the 7–11 age group. International in scope, these biographies cover a wide range of personalities—from historical figures to today's headliners—in such diverse fields as politics, the arts and sciences, athletics, and entertainment. Outstanding authors and illustrators present their subjects in a vividly anecdotal style, emphasizing the childhood and youth of each woman. More than a history lesson, the *WOMEN OF OUR TIME* books offer carefully documented life stories that will inform, entertain, and inspire the young people of our time.

"The author has—as she did in her biography of Rachel Carson—done a good job for pulling together facts about her subject, providing information about Low's role as founder of the Girl Scout movement as well as giving a picture of her as a person."
—Bulletin of the Center for Children's Books

JULIETTE GORDON LOW

AMERICA'S FIRST GIRL SCOUT

BY KATHLEEN V. KUDLINSKI

Illustrated by Sheila Hamanaka

PUFFIN BOOKS

For the wonderful girls of Troop 2135
(and all my "sisters" in
Girl Scouting)

K.V.K.

PUFFIN BOOKS
Published by the Penguin Group
Viking Penguin, a division of Penguin Books USA Inc.,
40 West 23rd Street, New York, New York 10010, U.S.A.
Penguin Books Ltd, 27 Wrights Lane, London W8 5TZ, England
Penguin Books Australia Ltd, Ringwood, Victoria, Australia
Penguin Books Canada Ltd, 2801 John Street, Markham, Ontario, Canada L3R 1B4
Penguin Books (N.Z.) Ltd, 182–190 Wairau Road, Auckland 10, New Zealand

Penguin Books Ltd, Registered Offices: Harmondsworth, Middlesex, England

First published in the United States of America by Viking Penguin,
a division of Penguin Books USA Inc., 1988
Published in Puffin Books 1989
1 3 5 7 9 10 8 6 4 2
Text copyright © Kathleen V. Kudlinski, 1988
Illustrations copyright © Sheila Hamanaka, 1988
All rights reserved

WOMEN OF OUR TIME ® is a registered trademark of Viking Penguin,
a division of Penguin Books USA Inc.

LIBRARY OF CONGRESS CATALOGING-IN-PUBLICATION DATA
Kudlinski, Kathleen V.   Juliette Gordon Low : America's first Girl Scout /
Kathleen V. Kudlinski ; illustrated by Sheila Hamanaka.   p.   cm. — (Women of our time)
Reprint. Originally published: New York : Viking Kestrel, 1988.
Summary: An illustrated biography of the founder of the Girl Scout
movement in the United States.
ISBN 0-14-032691-X
1. Low, Juliette Gordon, 1860–1927—Juvenile literature.   2. Girl
Scouts—United States—Biography—Juvenile literature.   3. Girl
Scouts of the United States of America—Biography—Juvenile
literature.   [1. Low, Juliette Gordon, 1860–1927.   2. Girl Scouts
of the United States of America—Biography.]   I. Hamanaka, Sheila,
ill. II. Title. III. Series.
HS3268.2.L68K83   1989   369.463'092—dc20   [B]   [92]   89-33681

Printed in the United States of America
Set in Garamond #3

CONTENTS

JULIETTE GORDON LOW
AMERICA'S FIRST GIRL SCOUT

1

She's a Daisy

"I've got something for the girls of Savannah, and all America, and all the world," Juliette Low told a good friend, "and we're going to start it tonight!" Her voice was full of excitement as she shared her plans to start Girl Scout troops all over the country.

Her friend thought it was just another of Daisy's crazy ideas. Daisy's family was used to her sudden, wild plans. They even teased about her "Girl Scoots."

But Daisy fooled them all. Within days, there were 18 Girl Scouts in America. In fifteen years, there were nearly 168,000. By the time you read this, more than

53 million people have belonged to Daisy's "Girl Scoots."

How did one woman start something so big and so important? And why didn't anybody think she could do it?

From the very beginning, Daisy Low's life was unusual. She was born in Savannah, Georgia, on Halloween night, October 31, 1860. Her name was Juliette Magill Kinzie Gordon, but nobody called her that. When her uncle saw the new baby girl, he said, "I bet she'll be a daisy!" After that, everyone called her Daisy.

Daisy had been born at the beginning of the terrible Civil War. Americans were killing other Americans. People from the south wanted a place where they could own slaves to do their work. People from the North, the Yankees, made laws against this. In the "War Between the States," Southerners fought to make a whole new country of their part of America so they could keep their slaves. The Yankees fought to stop them.

Daisy's father was a Southerner. He was away fighting Yankees most of the time. Little Daisy saw him at home only when he was hurt. She remembered helping to change his bandages. Then he would be off to war again. Except for a few years of college in Connecticut, Mr. Gordon had always lived in the South. His cotton business was there. His house, his slaves, and his daughters were Southern, too. But his wife, Nellie, was a Yankee.

Nellie Kinzie, Daisy's mother, met William Gordon in the North where they were both students. Her family was from Chicago, Illinois. There was no fighting there, so they wanted Nellie to bring the children home to be safe. Nothing was more important to Nellie than her husband. She stayed in Savannah to be near William.

Life was very hard in Georgia. Because of the war, Daisy never seemed to have enough to eat. She had never tasted sugar or cream or chicken. Every extra bit of food had to go to the soldiers. So did any money that could be spared. All of Daisy's clothes were old and shabby.

It was easy for Daisy to hate Yankees. Yankee soldiers were trying to kill her papa. Everyone she knew hated them. They said the Yankee leader, President Lincoln, was evil. And that General Sherman, who led the Yankee soldiers in Georgia, was the devil himself.

Then suddenly everything Daisy had learned was turned upside down. The Yankees captured Savannah. The streets were filled with Northern soldiers. It was awful and exciting at the same time. Years later, Daisy said, "I can even now feel the thrill and hear the tramp of the tired troops," when "I saw for the

3

first time real, live Yankees, thousands and thousands of them."

Worst of all, General Sherman came to Daisy's house. Daisy learned that he was friends with her grandparents in the North! General Sherman invited Daisy onto his lap, and gave the Gordon girls their very first taste of sugar. Daisy tried to remember her manners, but she couldn't forget that these men were enemies.

One of the soldiers with Sherman had been horribly wounded in the fighting. "I 'spect my papa did it," Daisy bragged, staring at him. "He's shot lots of Yankees." Her mother rushed Daisy from the room before she could say more.

There was so much hate and danger in Savannah now that women and children were ordered to leave. After saying goodbye to her husband, Mrs. Gordon hurried out of the city with six-year-old Ellie, four-year-old Daisy, and the new baby, Alice. As they got on the train, Daisy sang a nasty song that she and her friends always sang about Northerners.

The Gordon girls were small and weak even before they began the long trip to Chicago. Food was hard to get on the dirty, cold trains they had to ride. It was winter, and they had no warm clothes.

Uncle George, Mrs. Gordon's brother, met them in New York City. He was a Yankee, but he had

brought warm coats for everyone. When Daisy finally met her Yankee grandparents in Chicago, she couldn't help but like them. Her grandfather loved Daisy's mother so much. Her grandmother had parrots and puppies. How could they be enemies? It was confusing.

So was Daisy's first sight of snow. One morning soon after they got to Chicago, the Gordon girls awoke to a world covered with fresh white flakes. Daisy thought it was Yankee sugar—until she fell into a cold wet snowdrift!

It was wonderful to have enough food and warmth and sleep at last. But it was almost too late for Daisy. The long, hard trip had made her body weak. Daisy caught brain fever and became so sick the doctor thought she might die. When she began to get better, he said that if anything upset her, Daisy might get sick again. For months, Daisy got anything she asked for. The other children had to let her win every fight. Nobody dared to say "No" to her.

At long last, she was able to enjoy life at the Kinzies.' And what a life it was! The front lawn was often full of brightly dressed American Indians. They were there to talk with Daisy's grandfather about the white man's government. Mr. Kinzie could speak seventeen different Indian languages. He was always honest and fair with them, so he had no Indian enemies.

Mrs. Kinzie told exciting stories about the old days when the white men fought with Indians. Daisy's favorite was about her own great-grandmother, who had been stolen as a little girl by Indians. She was so full of energy that the tribe gave her the name "Little-Ship-Under-Full-Sail." They treated her like a princess. She grew to love them and to think of herself as an Indian. For four years, she dressed in leather and lived in the woods. The Indians cared for her so

much that they gave her the nicest gift they could. They gave her back to her own family.

Daisy asked to hear that story over and over. The Gordons started calling her "Little-Ship," too. Though she was still skinny and small for a five-year-old, Daisy was now as full of energy and fun as that little white Indian girl. She had learned that she could get what she wanted. She also had seen that enemies could be friends if you were honest and fair and really got to know them. By the time it was safe to go home, Daisy had changed a lot. So had Savannah.

2

Twenty Cousins

The South was a sad place for grown-ups after the war. Like many others, Mr. Gordon had lost all his money. His cotton business was ruined. What would he do? Mrs. Gordon sold some land she owned in the North and gave the money to her husband. It let them keep their grand home. Mr. Gordon could start a new business. And there was money to pay the few ex-slaves and servants who had stayed at the end of the war.

For the Gordon children, it was an exciting time. They watched as, bit by bit, their house became beautiful again. The front columns were freshly painted. Trash was cleared from the courtyard. Silver that had been hidden from the Yankees was polished and put back on the tables. Black paint that had covered the glowing wooden doors was scraped away.

As Mr. Gordon's business slowly grew, new china was bought to replace the set stolen during the war. The girls could have prettier dresses. And there were new animals in the stable.

Daisy dearly loved the animals. If an animal was in need, she would do anything to help it. Once she jumped into a muddy stream to save a drowning cat. She didn't stop to think that she might be in danger. She seldom thought about what might happen before she did anything.

One night, she was worried about her favorite cow. Daisy knew it was freezing cold in the barn. She snuck out of the house and wrapped a good blanket around the cow. In the morning, her father found the blanket, stamped into the muck of the barn floor. Daisy got a scolding, but the cow had been warm!

Now there were two boys and four girls in Daisy's family. The sisters and brothers did everything together, including going to school. At Miss Blois' school, Daisy learned to read from a book called *Little Tales for Very Little Children*. All the words in the book had three letters to make it easy. Daisy read about "Sam and his Dog," "Red Leg," and "Bob and Tom Lee."

Miss Blois also began teaching Daisy to speak French, to behave with the best manners, and to understand history and geography. Daisy didn't like spelling or arithmetic, so she wouldn't learn them. Sometimes, when the teacher told her to work on her spelling, Daisy drew pictures instead. She loved art more than anything else at school.

But most of all, she loved the summertime. Then the Gordons all went to Aunt Eliza's home in north Georgia. Twenty cousins lived with their parents, aunts, and uncles in the huge house by the Etowah River. One of them said, "We spent our lives out-of-doors. . . . Back of the house were the rose gardens and the fruit orchards," and beyond, "miles of tall pines."

The children ate breakfast in the house, then scattered over the plantation, playing Indian and Settler in the woods, princesses on "castle rock," or making paper dolls in the tiny schoolhouse. They often gave plays for the grown-ups. Daisy was the best actress. She remembered her lines well and loved dressing up in fancy clothes.

One summer, she started a club called the "Helpful Hands." Her sisters and cousins were members. Daisy thought they should all learn to sew and make clothes for the poor. She would be their sewing teacher. The

only problem was that Daisy didn't know anything about sewing! She made the club members thread needles with their left hands and all the clothes they made fell apart. Daisy's brother Arthur teased them, calling the club the "Helpless Hands."

They swam in the Etowah River on hot days. Young ladies never wore swimsuits in the 1860s. They swam in shoes, petticoats, blouses, and bathing skirts that came below their knees. It was hard to swim in all those clothes. Once, after nine-year-old Daisy went swimming, she saw a little girl fall into the water. Though Daisy had changed back into dry clothes, she jumped in and saved the girl. Daisy never talked about her good deeds. If she hadn't had to explain how her dress got wet, no one would have known about her quick thinking.

Daisy's deeds weren't *all* good ones. While they were making taffy one day, a cousin told Daisy that her hair was just the color of the sticky candy. She told him to braid some of it into her long hair to see if he was right. He was. But that hair, and the candy, had to be cut off. For months, Daisy's pointed face, her sharp little freckled nose, and her big brown eyes were framed by a shaggy mop of pale brown hair.

As the cousins got older, they played different games. For five summers, they wrote and illustrated a magazine. It always had some of Daisy's clever drawings, poems, and stories. When she was eight or nine, she wrote "The Piggy," a poem about a lazy young pig. Daisy's Piggy told his Mama that all he ever wanted was to live in a garbage heap. At that, his Mama bit his tail until it bled. Then poor Piggy promised he'd never be lazy again!

Another summer, Daisy and her sister Nellie made paper dolls of the people from *Little Women*, a book by Louisa May Alcott. They worked for days, drawing, and cutting, and painting the dolls and their clothes. Daisy was good at all kinds of art, but she never practiced anything long enough to become an artist. Her family started calling her "grasshopper" because she was always jumping into new hobbies, new ideas, or new games.

In those lazy years, Daisy wasn't doing anything about her future. She already knew what she would be when she grew up. She would be a *lady*. Like all the other women in her family, Daisy would marry a rich man and live in a beautiful house. Other women had to work, to cook and clean and care for children. The ladies Daisy knew had enough money to pay others to do these things for them.

There were some things that ladies did have to know. They had to have perfect manners, speak other languages, and be able to talk about almost anything with anyone. Miss Blois taught only young children in Savannah. To learn the social skills she would need, 14-year-old Daisy had to go away to a boarding school where she would live all winter. Daisy could be lazy no more. Ready or not, it was time she became a lady.

3

Becoming a Lady

From the moment she got to school in Virginia, Daisy was homesick. Her greatest loves were family and fun. There wasn't much of either at Stuart Hall School. Daisy knew her parents couldn't afford train tickets to bring her home on vacations. She wouldn't see them again for nine long months.

Ellie, Daisy's older sister, was at Stuart Hall, too. She and Daisy pushed their beds close together, but they weren't allowed to talk after "lights out" at night. And when the sisters did get to talk in the daytime, they could speak only in French or German. It was good practice for learning another language, but it didn't help Daisy's homesickness.

In Georgia, Daisy had spent hours outdoors every day. She loved climbing trees, racing through the woods, riding, and swimming. The Stuart Hall girls had to walk around slowly and quietly, and always in pairs. It was a very dull fall for Daisy.

For her birthday, Daisy's mother sent a Bible with covers made of red alligator skin. Reading it made Daisy feel closer to her parents. She learned dozens of verses by heart. Whenever she had a problem, Daisy reached for that Bible. She would close her eyes, spread the red covers, and put her finger somewhere on the open page. She believed that the verse she was pointing to would tell her what to do.

At Stuart Hall, the teachers were always telling her to be gentle, good, and quiet. At home, everyone was used to Daisy's funny tricks and the silly troubles she got herself into. Her mother always laughed and called them "Daisy's stunts." The teachers didn't laugh at all. "Mama," Daisy wrote in a letter, "I can't keep all the rules. I'm too much like you. I'll keep clear of the big scrapes, but little ones I can't avoid."

Daisy did such funny things that she soon had many friends. One time she heard that white spots on fingernails were ugly. She had spots like that. A lady's magazine had a recipe to take spots away. Daisy tried it. Instead of taking the spots off, the gooey mess made Daisy's fingers stick to the bowl! It took hours of soaking in hot water before she could wiggle them free.

As the year went by, Daisy stopped being so unhappy. The school held parties for the girls. The parties were for practicing manners, but they were fun, too. At the first costume party, the girls guessed right away who Daisy was. It was easy. She was the shortest girl in the school. She had been short and skinny since her sickness in Chicago. For the next party, she wore a tall hat so she would look as big as the other girls. That time, no one guessed who she was.

Daisy got used to the hard classwork and strict rules. Art was still her favorite class, but by the spring, all her schoolwork was going well. She even looked forward to going back to Stuart Hall the next year.

In the summer, Daisy and her sisters practiced walking with teacups on their heads. They knew that ladies should move smoothly and gracefully. At 15, Daisy had good posture, but she was not pretty. Her nose and chin were very pointed. Pulling her hair back tightly just made her look worse. As she got older, though, Daisy got prettier.

A year later, she changed boarding schools. Daisy's little sister, Alice, studied with her at Edge Hill School in Virginia. Ellie had gone away to study in New York City. Daisy liked Edge Hill much better than Stuart Hall School. The rules were not as hard and she was getting better at following them.

There was more fun at Edge Hill, too. Daisy joined a club, the Theta Taus. They held secret meetings and had special feasts. She saved money for weeks to buy a club pin. She took riding lessons. Riding side-saddle was one of the few sports ladies were allowed in the 1870s. And all ladies were expected to draw or paint well. Daisy had a real talent for art. When a roommate asked her what she liked best about school, Daisy answered, "Painting—it is my *greatest* joy."

Every month, report cards were sent home. If the classwork and behavior grades were all good, the cards were written in gold ink. Daisy got several "Golden Reports," but she was the only one to win a silver medal for drawing.

Daisy was also winning confidence. She had lived away from home for several years. She had learned to be friendly with many different kinds of people. And she had begun to like boys. After a dance she wrote, "At first I was awfully scared, but as soon as I was introduced, I went in heart and soul, and never had a better time in my life." At 17, Daisy was ready for finishing school.

In a way, a finishing school was like a college, for it finished the training a girl would need to be a lady. Daisy was sent to the Charbonniers' school in New York City. A school friend remembered, "We not only talked nothing but French" at Charbonniers', "we dressed like French girls in black aprons all day long to keep our dresses clean." They were never allowed to talk to boys. They weren't even supposed to look at any boys they passed on the street. It was hard, but Daisy followed the rules.

Life there wasn't all work. There were trips to museums, and evenings at operas, plays, and concerts. The school had singing lessons and drawing classes. On Saturdays, all the girls went to the elegant Dods-

worth Dancing Academy. They didn't just learn to dance there. They also studied ballroom manners and learned how to curtsey. They learned how to sit gracefully in a ball gown, with both feet resting gently on the floor. They could never cross their legs.

Daisy loved all of it. She asked Alice to come and share the fun at Charbonniers'. Alice didn't want to go all the way to New York. Mrs. Gordon made Alice go with Daisy in 1881. Alice was homesick and unhappy. Early in December, she caught scarlet fever. Soon she was too sick to go home. She was even too ill for Daisy to see her. After Christmas, Alice died.

The Gordon family was heartbroken. Mrs. Gordon felt worst of all, for she was the one who had sent Alice to Charbonniers'. She thought it was her fault that Alice had died.

Daisy felt awful, too. She had told Alice it would be such fun at the school. Reading the Bible helped Daisy feel better about Alice. But nothing seemed to help the way her mother felt. She wanted the Gordon family to act sad about Alice all the time. For years, she got angry with anyone who seemed happy.

Mr. Gordon's business was going very well. He could afford to send Daisy and the other children traveling to happier places. Now that they weren't away at boarding school, they visited cousins' and friends' houses and traveled to England.

At last, Daisy's schooling was done. It was time for her "coming out" in Savannah. This special ceremony marks the moment when a girl is finally a lady. Daisy was nervous. The ballroom was full of the most important ladies and gentlemen of Savannah. Her date reached for her arm and led her to the doorway. Everyone turned to look. A loud voice announced, "Miss Juliette Magill Kinzie Gordon." Daisy curt-

seyed and walked gracefully into the ballroom as a grown-up lady.

Everything had gone just as planned. Daisy's training was done. She was ready for a handsome young man to marry her and sweep her away to a land of fairy-tale castles and princesses. And that is exactly what happened. But Daisy did not live happily ever after.

4

"Scotch Weather"

Daisy was entering the happiest time of her life, and she looked it. Her brown eyes sparkled with laughter. Her hair was tied loosely and her face looked soft and happy. Her life was full of buggy rides and balls, picnics and parties, boating and horse-riding. With her wit and looks, she was one of the most popular girls in Savannah. Several men asked her to marry them.

One of the men she liked most was William Low, a handsome and rich young man. Daisy had met Willie in England on her travels after Alice died. In 1882, Daisy told a school friend that she was "madly and unreasonably in love with him." Daisy wanted to have a long marriage like her parents, full of children and love. Was this the right man for her? When she finally did decide to marry Willie, she kept their plans secret. Daisy's mother was still too upset from Alice's death to think it was good news.

Daisy's health had been poor since her illness in Chicago. One Sunday morning, she awoke with an earache. She had read that putting silver nitrate in an ear would end the pain. She told her doctor how to do it. He didn't like the idea at all. Daisy argued, "If you don't put it in, I'll get someone else to do it for me." Her doctor finally agreed.

It hurt as he did it. By the time she got home, the pain was so awful that even she knew it was a mistake. She lay in bed for days as the silver nitrate slowly ruined her ear. When she was well enough to get up, she could barely hear on that side.

Again Daisy was traveling. She came home for her sister Ellie's wedding in 1884. For the first time since Alice's death, Mrs. Gordon began to be her old, jolly self. It was time, Daisy thought, to tell the truth about Willie. His father died soon after, leaving Willie millions of dollars and the family businesses.

Daisy was 26 when they were finally married in 1886. She chose the day of her mother and father's wedding for her own, December 21. She carried lilies

of the valley, Alice's favorite flower. All eight brides-
maids dressed in white, and each wore a gift from
Willie: a diamond-covered pin in the shape of a daisy.
Willie had chosen a crescent moon and star made of
diamonds to give to his bride. As they left for their
honeymoon, friends cheered and threw rice for luck.

Daisy shook her head and ran to the carriage. By
the next morning, her good ear hurt. She tried not to
fuss, but it got worse. Willie had to take Daisy back
to Savannah to see a doctor. A rice grain had fallen
into her ear and caused an infection. It would have

to come out. Something went wrong in the operation, and Daisy's good ear was ruined.

Now she could barely hear at all. Daisy set off for England, nearly deaf and frightened. How could she hear a fire alarm? How could she talk to people when she couldn't hear what they were saying? How would she know when to laugh at a joke? It was hard, but she never complained.

Daisy's only job in England was to have fun—there were 18 servants to help her get dressed, serve her meals and do the housework. Like many of their wealthy friends in the 1880s, Daisy and Willie owned four homes.

Their country house was near the home of Rudyard Kipling. Daisy became great friends with the writer of *Rikki-Tikki-Tavi* and the *Jungle Books*. They both liked to do silly things. One night after a formal dinner, Daisy invited him to go fishing. Rudyard ended up rolling in the wet grass struggling to get a trout out of the water. Daisy slipped down the muddy slope to the stream in her ballgown.

Daisy loved being in the center of all the social life. She told wonderful jokes and stories at parties. That way, she didn't have to strain to hear what others were saying. She had her cook make meals from the American South, using Virginia ham, peanuts, and corn. Londoners were delighted by the taste of these new foods. Daisy rode beautifully during hunting season. And she was friendly with everyone.

In England, ladies were presented at court instead of having a coming-out ceremony. When she went to meet the Queen, Daisy wore a white satin dress covered with ostrich feathers. Diamond pins "glittered like the Milky Way through the feathers." Her dress had a thick bustle in back and a train lined with pink silk dragging far behind on the floor.

There was a long line to get to the throne room. When Daisy got tired of carrying both her heavy train and an armful of flowers, she just set her flowers on the bustle of the lady in front of her. The poor woman never knew she was carrying them!

During her first hunting season, Daisy and her horse did too much jumping. Her back had been hurt before, and now she was told she could never ride again. What would she do while the others were out hunting? "I can hardly face the loneliness of the coming winter now that I cannot ride any more," she complained.

Daisy filled her empty time with painting, making clay statues, and metalworking. Every week, Daisy secretly visited a poor old woman who lived nearby. The villagers thought the woman was dangerously ill. They wouldn't go near her. Daisy read to the woman for hours and brought her food and cheered her up.

Things were not very cheerful for Daisy. Both she

and Willie wanted to have many children. She never told anyone what was wrong, but when she came back from a hospital visit soon after her marriage, she knew she could never have children.

She filled her empty house with pets. Her favorite for years was a fussy little Pekingese dog. Like her grandmother back in Chicago, Daisy collected parrots. Blue Boy, a colorful macaw, often rode on her shoulder. She even kept pet mockingbirds from America to keep her company. She needed them all.

Willie always left her at home when he went hunting. Now he began taking long trips without her, too. And he began drinking too much alcohol. That kind of drinking can change a person, and Willie was beginning to change. He is like "Scotch weather," Daisy once told her brother Arthur. "When he is bad, he is awful, but when really nice, sweeter than summer." When Willie was drunk, he teased her by talking so softly that she couldn't hope to hear him. When he wasn't drinking, he would give her diamonds. Daisy kept this, like her illnesses, secret. Not even her family knew.

Daisy had visited them in Savannah every year. In 1898, America was at war again, fighting to help Cuba, an island near Florida. Spain owned the island and wouldn't let the Cubans be free. Daisy came home to help nurse the Spanish-American War soldiers

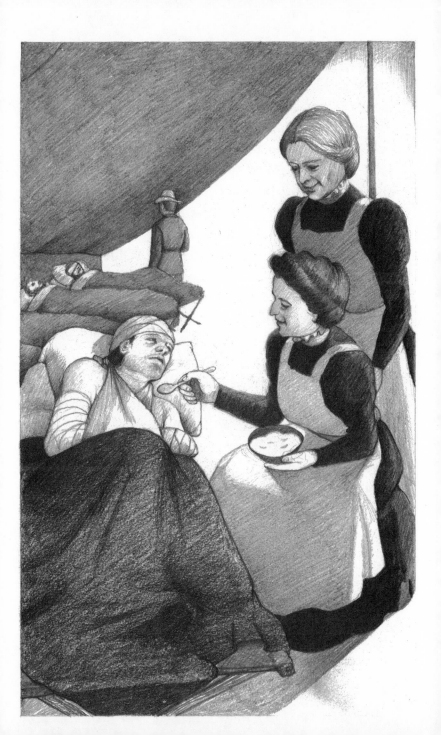

who were wounded or sick with tropical fevers.

She and her mother left their servants behind and spent the hot summer in Florida, living in tents and cooking over wood fires. It was hard to find food the sickest men could eat, until Nellie found a supply of baby food. She called it pudding, and they liked it until they found out what it really was. Then Daisy put some rum in to change the flavor. "You can't say that *this* is for babies!" she joked.

When Daisy got home, things with Willie were far worse. She still loved him very much, but the more he drank, the less he loved her. In 1905, Willie died, sickened by years of drinking. He left his homes and money to others. Daisy got nothing.

She wasn't mad at him. She was full of sorrow. For the rest of her life, Daisy would say to friends now and then, "Something nice is going to happen today. . . . I dreamed of Willie last night."

At age 45, Daisy's poor hearing was getting even worse. She had lost the man she loved and the dream she had lived for. She had no money. No home. No job. No children. What would she do with the rest of her life?

5

"Little Stars"

After years of owning four homes, Daisy now had to live with friends. Her father even sent her an allowance as he did when she was a schoolgirl. Months later, the courts decided that Daisy should have at least a part of Willie's wealth and all of his American properties. Now she had a house in Savannah and enough money for an English home and some travel.

Daisy wandered from country to country for seven years. Often she took a young niece or cousin along on her journeys. Once she sent a telegram inviting Eleanor, a friend's daughter, to join her on a trip to

Egypt. Eleanor had to hurry—the boat was leaving in just three days! On the long sail to Egypt, Daisy worked for hours every morning, carving a clay statue of Eleanor's head. When they finally got there, Daisy threw her work into the ocean. It wasn't good enough, she explained.

In Egypt, they climbed the Great Pyramids, drank gallons of strong Turkish coffee, went shopping, and rode donkeys through deserts of yellow sand. Long after Eleanor was worn out, Daisy was looking for more excitement.

Daisy made friends with everyone she met on her trips. "To know her at all was to want to know her better," Eleanor explained. "And to know her better was easy because she was so interested in you, whoever you were."

No matter where she was traveling in the world, Daisy always came home to Savannah for Christmas. The children loved her visits. She brought strange, exciting gifts from far-off lands for everyone. Polly Poons, an African parrot, rode her shoulder and screamed, "Coming! Coming!" whenever the phone rang.

But it was Daisy herself, not the gifts or the parrot, that the children adored most. Her face had started to look strained from trying so hard to hear, but she was a lot of fun. When one of her nephews was ill,

Daisy spent hours by his bed, showing him how to make things out of paper. She dressed up with the children in fantastic costumes. Sometimes she let them try her big hearing aid. With its point in their ear, they could aim the horn-shaped end across the room and hear every whisper. Other times, Daisy made up funny games they all could play together. Then, when they were tired, she told stories about the places she had visited.

Other people were telling stories about Daisy, too. She had bought one of the first cars in Savannah, but she was such a terrible driver that people pulled their carriages off the road when they saw her coming. One day, she crashed right into a house. Her car ended up in the dining room where a family was sitting at the table, eating a meal. When her brother Bill asked what she said to them, Daisy answered, "Why, I didn't say anything. I didn't think it would be polite to bother them while they were eating!"

Daisy's entire life was changed as she sat at a meal a few years later in England. A famous war hero, Sir Robert Baden-Powell, was sitting next to her. England had been fighting against Dutch settlers in English Africa. Major General Baden-Powell had helped his men win battles, even though many of them were sick and starving. Daisy and Sir Robert found that they had a lot to talk about besides his fame. Both of them enjoyed sculpture. Both had family stories about adventures on the American frontier. Both of them sketched whenever they could.

Daisy liked him very much. They spent a lot of time together during the spring. Her deafness made no difference to Sir Robert. They grew very close, but Daisy said she would not marry him. She felt he should have a younger wife, a woman who could give him children.

Like Daisy, he loved young people. He told her about his new club, the Boy Scouts. In his battles, Sir

Robert had asked African boys to help the soldiers. The boys didn't fight, but carried messages, found food, and spied on the enemy instead. They needed to know camping and tracking skills, first aid, and flag signals. Sir Robert felt English boys should be prepared to help in case of war, too.

In Scouts, boys didn't just learn useful skills. They played games, went camping, and practiced being helpful, honest, and fair. Because he was a national hero and because scouting was such fun, more boys were joining every day.

Sir Robert had done so much good in the world that it made Daisy feel that she had led "a wasted life." Finally she told him how useless he was making her feel. He said gently that she could still do something worthwhile. What could she do? she wondered. "There are little stars that guide us on," he told her, "although we do not realize it."

Just being a fine lady wasn't enough for Daisy anymore. She began to think about what she liked and what she was good at. As a girl, she had learned how to sit gracefully and how to read French. She had never learned how to make a difference in the world.

Sir Robert told Daisy about Girl Guides. His sister, Agnes, had started the club in 1910. Like Boy Scouting, Girl Guiding taught skills that were really useful—skills Daisy wished she had learned. She liked

"The Guides' Law," from a Girl Guide book Agnes and Sir Robert had written. It told girls "to be Loyal, Kind, Obedient, and Cheerful."

Daisy was so excited about Guiding that she wrote home about it: "Dear Papa, I like girls and I like the organization and the rules and pastimes, so if you find that I get very deeply interested, you must not be surprised."

Daisy started a troop near her home in Scotland. Only seven girls could come from the poor farms nearby. One had to walk six miles to get to the meetings at Daisy's house on Saturday afternoons. The Girl Guides were welcomed with a grand, rich dinner. They played games and did such interesting projects that they kept coming. Together they learned knot-tying, cooking, and first aid from Daisy or from her friends.

When Daisy found out that all her girls would soon have to go to work in a distant city, she was angry. They were much too young to leave home! If money was the problem, she would start a troop project so they could earn it right there.

She taught them how to raise chickens to sell to the wealthy people who lived in the hunting lodges. Then they learned to spin yarn from sheep's wool. At the end of the fall season, Daisy returned to London and found a shop that would buy the yarn they made. Now the girls could grow up in their own homes.

Daisy had made a huge difference in their lives in just a few short months!

She had seen Girl Guiding at work in the country. But would it work for city girls? The next winter, she started another troop in the slums of London. At first, the girls came for the free meals Daisy served as snacks. Soon they came because they loved Guiding and they loved Daisy. They learned the same skills as her Scottish Guides, wore the same pins, and had just as much fun. She started another troop but knew she would be going to the United States soon. The girls needed a new leader.

She told Rose Kerr, a woman she had met and liked, to take the troop. Mrs. Kerr was surprised. "I cannot possibly do it," she answered. "I have no time. I do not live in London. I am no good with girls."

Nobody had said "No" to Daisy when she was a small, sick child. No one would say it now, either. Daisy pretended to be too deaf to hear what Mrs. Kerr was saying. She just smiled and said, "Then that is settled. The next meeting is on Thursday and I have told them you will take it." Mrs. Kerr was a fine leader, just as Daisy had known she would be.

Daisy had seen how Girl Guiding could help children. She knew how to interest the girls and she knew how to get leaders for them. It was time for her to take Girl Guiding to the United States. She sailed for America on January 6, 1912.

Sir Robert Baden-Powell happened to be on the same boat. A lovely young lady they met aboard, Olave Soames, said that "whether Daisy was lying in her cabin or walking or sitting up on deck, she was hard at work, thinking, talking, and planning."

Before Daisy had unpacked her trunks in Savannah, she was on the phone asking the first of her friends to help. "I've got something for Savannah, and all America, and all the world," she began. . . .

6

"Ask the Girls"

On March 12, 1912, Daisy held the first official Girl Guide meeting in the United States. She showed the books, badges, and uniforms that her English girls had used. It sounded like such fun that the Savannah girls begged her to start a troop right then. Seventeen 12-year-olds signed up. Daisy wrote her niece's name, Daisy Gordon, at the top of the list. Her niece was out of town, but Daisy was sure she would enjoy the club when she got home. She was right. Young Daisy loved Guiding.

They all did. The girls met every Saturday at Daisy's

house. They ate the healthy snacks that Daisy said should be part of every meeting. They tried new skills. If a girl could pass a test on the skills, she was given a badge to wear. At a meeting, they might practice bathing a baby doll for the child-nurse badge, learning to know ten kinds of snakes for a nature badge, or making a chair by tying sticks together for a camping badge.

Sometimes there was a hike or bird walk for exercise. Other weeks, the girls changed into big, loose bloomer shorts to play basketball. This was very exciting because young Southern ladies never wore pants in those days. The Guides covered their shocking bloomers with long coats before they walked outdoors to the basketball court. Then they pulled great canvas curtains around the court before they took off their coats. That way, no one walking by would see their legs.

Daisy did not stay for many meetings. She dearly loved the girls but her job was to organize troops, not lead them. Off across the country she went, talking everywhere about the Girl Guides. She could always pick out the right person for each leadership job, and get the woman to agree. "Somehow she could never hear the word 'No,' even if it was shouted at her," an early leader remembered.

And it was off to England again to visit her Guides there. In September of 1912, she got sad news. Her papa had died. He was the one who gave lively Mrs. Gordon and Daisy some sense of calm. He had always helped them out with money and advice when their lives got out of control.

Mrs. Gordon lost her interest in life again, the way she had after Alice's death. Daisy had also just learned that Sir Robert Baden-Powell was going to marry Olave Soames. Daisy, sad and disappointed, went into hiding. She claimed she was being treated for back pain. For three months, she didn't even answer letters from her dear brothers and sisters.

When she was ready to come out smiling, Daisy headed home to her Guides in America. She began planning a National Girl Guide organization for the United States. She would be president, of course. In June of 1913, her National Office opened in Washington, D.C.

There were already a few troops of Girl Scouts in the States, led by women who had seen Boy Scouts in England. Daisy wanted those troops in her National Organization, too. She changed the name "Girl Guides" to "Girl Scouts" to make it easy for the others to join.

The Boy Scouts had Sir Robert's book and the Girl Guides had Agnes' handbook to teach them. Daisy's girls needed a book, too. She asked William Hoxie to write it. He had led groups like Scouts in Savannah and he had more time to write than Daisy. When he was done, Daisy worked on it for a weekend and finished the handbook. She called it *How Girls Can Help Their Country*. She had changed parts to make it better for her girls.

The book taught many skills, for "times may come when you will have to . . . milk, cook, cut wood, act as a nurse, or even defend your own life." There were electrician, drummer, and clerk badges to earn, as well as homemaking badges. Think about becoming a doctor or aviator, it said, but don't try to be like a boy, for "It is better to be a real girl such as no boy can possibly be."

In the book, Daisy asked each girl to promise three things:

1. To do your duty to God and to your country,
2. To help other people at all times,
3. To obey the laws of the Scouts.

The Ten Laws told the girls to be honest, useful, helpful, to be a friend to animals, to be cheerful and thrifty, a friend to all and a sister to every other Girl Scout. The book also told girls to be strong and healthy and to spend lots of time outdoors.

The Savannah troop complained to Daisy that being outdoors in Georgia's reddish dirt stained their uniforms. They had made dresses of blue to match the English Girl Guide uniforms. Boy Scouts everywhere wore tan. The Savannah girls thought that tan fabric would work better for them, too.

"Ask the girls," Daisy always said when a problem came up. "They'll know what's best." The uniforms were changed to tan. Asking the girls was a new idea in 1913. At that time, children were always told what to do. Nobody thought they had enough sense to make their own choices. Nobody, that is, except Daisy.

She always wore her scout uniform. A friend thought she did it just to make the girls feel good. Soon she realized that Daisy really "*loved* that big hat; she *loved* that ridiculous whistle; she *loved* her whole uniform.

She wasn't wearing them, as some of us were, because it seemed best; *she loved to wear them.*"

Once, at a lunch with other rich ladies, Daisy also wore a hat trimmed with real fruit and raw carrots. Whenever someone asked why she had done such a silly thing, Daisy was ready. She said she couldn't afford a new hat because she had given every extra penny she had to the Girl Scouts. Then she would say that her wonderful girls could still use a bit more money. Daisy's stunt worked. Many of the women gave her money, smiling as they did.

In 1917, America entered a World War. Daisy sent a telegram to the President of the United States to offer the help of her Girl Scouts. Only Daisy could have known how much help her girls would be. They raised food, helped the Red Cross, prepared bandages and Christmas packages for soldiers, raised money for the government, and cared for younger children whose mothers worked in factories.

In the middle of the war, Daisy's mother died. Daisy had no time to hide in sorrow. Her Girl Scouts were making 500 sandwiches a day to feed soldiers traveling through Washington. They were growing beans in Boston's fancy parks. More and more girls joined to help in the Scouts' war work. Younger girls wanted

to be Girl Scouts, too. A "Junior" age level was added for six- to 10-year olds. Early in 1919, 150 new Girl Scouts were joining every day. Daisy sold her pearls and used that money to move the offices to a larger space in New York City.

As soon as the war was over, Daisy hurried back to England. People had called it "The War to End All Wars," for they were sure no one would ever want to fight again. Daisy's Girl Scouts had been such a help during wartime. Could they help in keeping peace, too? Daisy remembered her grandfather's friends, the Indians. He had taken the time to speak with them. She remembered that as a little child, she couldn't

think of Yankees as enemies once she got to know them.

If Daisy's Girl Scouts got to know other girls around the world, they would never allow wars with their new friends. In America, Daisy started the "International Post Office." There, girls could write letters back and forth to girls in far-off lands. In England, she helped Robert and Olave Baden-Powell start the World Association of Girl Guides and Girl Scouts.

For years, Daisy traveled back and forth across the Atlantic Ocean, keeping the friendship between Girl Scouts and Girl Guides strong. In 1920, the first International Conference was held in England. Girl Guides from 46 countries came or sent messages of peace and friendship.

When she got back home, Daisy had a hard decision to make. She knew she wasn't always easy to work with. She couldn't hear well. Her playful humor sometimes made it hard to hold meetings. Once, when the Girl Scout shoes were being chosen, Daisy stood on her head to show off the ones she was wearing! She cared so much about Scouting that it was hard for her to let others make decisions. When Daisy made up her mind, she didn't like to hear other ideas, unless they came from the girls.

Without this kind of strong leadership, Girl Scouting would never have grown so fast in the United States. But now Daisy was standing in the way of Scouting's growth, and she knew it. She wasn't feeling well. She wanted to spend what energy she had left on the girls worldwide. Sadly, she gave up being president, asking only to be called "Founder."

Several times in the next few years, Daisy went into hiding. This time, it wasn't because she was sad. She was really ill. Her face showed the strain of trying to hide the pain of cancer.

In 1925, Daisy hurried into the Girl Scout office. She told Jane Rippin, the director, that the next International Conference would be held at the new Girl Scout Camp in New York. Mrs. Rippin was speechless. Nothing had been built at Camp Macy. No buildings. No paths. No bathrooms. She told Daisy that it couldn't be finished in less than a year.

"Jane," Daisy said, putting her hand on her friend's shoulder, "if we don't have it next year, I won't be there." Now her secret was out. Daisy didn't have much longer to live. The women at the National Office said that for Daisy, they would do the impossible. Camp Macy would be ready.

And somehow it was. The women joked about having carpenters just finishing the back doors while guests were coming in the front. Daisy glowed with happiness as she led Robert and Olave Baden-Powell up a

path lined with flags from other lands. That night a giant bonfire lit the sky.

One by one, girls from many countries stepped up to the fire. Each one told about the gifts their country had given to the world, then threw a stick into the blaze. Daisy watched as sparks floated into the sky like thousands of little stars. She knew she had indeed made a difference—a difference that mattered around the world!

After one last trip to England, she came home to America. She was very weak, but she had to talk to her old Girl Scouting friends. She wanted them to know her ideas for the future of Girl Scouts.

The Girl Scout president sent Daisy a telegram from all the women at the National Office. It said. "You are not only the first Girl Scout, you are th best Girl Scout of them all." That was the nicest thin anyone could have said to Daisy. Later she looked around her room. It was crowded full of flowers from her friends. "If this keeps up," she said, grinning, "there won't be any flowers left for the funeral!"

A few days later, on January 17, 1927, Juliette Gordon Low died. Daisy was buried just as she wished, dressed in her Girl Scout uniform with the wonderful telegram tucked in her pocket.

ABOUT THIS BOOK

I believe there really are "little stars that guide us on." People we happen to meet, books we read, even the places we visit can change our lives forever. Girl Scouting, the work of Daisy Low, has been one of those guiding stars in millions of families like mine. My mother was my Girl Scout leader when I was young and now I am my daughter Betsy's leader.

Before I wrote this book, all I knew about Daisy was what the Girl Scout handbooks said. I needed to find out much more. At the National Girl Scout Headquarters in New York City, I got to see letters Daisy wrote. I read what Daisy's friends and family remembered about her. I read other books about "The Founder" and talked with very old scouts who had met Daisy long ago. I visited Savannah, Georgia, and Camp Edith Macy in Briarcliff Manor, New York.

The uniforms, badges, age levels, and wording of the promise and laws have all changed since 1912, but Daisy's basic ideas still guide three million Girl Scouts today.

K.V.K.